"Kimi ni Nare"

Hayaku otona ni naritai no ni, se wo kagameteita koro ga aru,
Hayaokuri mo makimodoshi mo dekinai toki wo, egakinagara ikiteiru
Hetakuso na kyou no jibun mo kesazu ni, ue kara aru ga mama o egakidasu dake
Otona ni nareba naruhodo sora ga takaku takaku kanjiru

Ima wa mada katenakute ii makeru imi wo shiru toki da
Ima wa mada wakaranakute ii muri ni nomikonde hakidashita nigai omoi
Ima wa mada dekinakute ii dekinai toki ni dake dekiru koto ga aru
Ima wa mada mayoeba ii dore wo erande mo kimi no kotae nanda to mune wo hatte ieru nara

Ima wa mada aenakute ii aenai bun dake tsuyoku omoereba ii
Ima wa mada mienakute ii mienai hodo taisetsu na kimochi nandarou
Ima wa mada kodoku de ii mada minu nakamatachi wo minna ima kodoku dakara
Ima wa mada soko ni ireba ii tsugi no basho wa jibun de kimerunda
Ima wa mada nani mo nakute ii karappo nara sunao ni nare
Ima wa mada sono mama de ii kawaranai mono mamoritsudukenagara kawareru nara

Sonna kimi ga suteki kadouka ? wo kimeru no wa kimi ja nai
Kimi wo ai suru hito ga miteru no wa ima yori mo zutto tooku no kimi

Dame na toki mo kagayaku toki mo onaji you ni kimi wo shinjiteru
Sono ai wa honmono dakara itsu no hi ka honmono no kimi ni nare

Ima wa mada katenakute ii wakaranakute ii dekinakute ii
Mayoeba ii aenakute ii ienakute ii kodoku de ii
Ima wa mada soko ni ireba ii nani mo nakute ii sono mama de ii
Itsu no hi ka honmono no kimi ni nare
Kimi ni nare kimi ni nare

Well, see you in Volume 2!

SEVEN SEAS ENTERTAINMENT PRESENTS

Become You

story and art by Ichigo Takano

VOL. 1

TRANSLATION
Amber Tamosaitis

ADAPTATION
Claudie Summers

LETTERING
Lys Blakeslee

COVER DESIGN
KC Fabellon

PROOFREADER
Danielle King
Holly Kolodziejczak

ASSISTANT EDITOR
Jenn Grunigen

EDITOR
Shannon Fay

PRODUCTION MANAGER
Lissa Pattillo

MANAGING EDITOR
Julie Davis

EDITOR-IN-CHIEF
Adam Arnold

PUBLISHER
Jason DeAngelis

Become You: Kimi ni Nare Vol. 1

First published in Japan in 2018 by Futabasha Publishers Ltd., Tokyo.
English version published by Seven Seas Entertainment.
Under license from Futabasha Publishers Ltd.

Seven Seas press and purchase enquiries can be sent to Marketing Manager Lianne Sentar at press@gomanga.com. Information regarding the distribution and purchase of digital editions is available from Digital Manager CK Russell at digital@gomanga.com.

ISBN: 978-1-64275-685-2

Printed in Canada

First Printing: September 2019

10 9 8 7 6 5 4 3 2 1

FOLLOW US ONLINE: ***www.sevenseasentertainment.com***

READING DIRECTIONS

This book reads from ***right to left***, Japanese style. If this is your first time reading manga, you start reading from the top right panel on each page and take it from there. If you get lost, just follow the numbered diagram here. It may seem backwards at first, but you'll get the hang of it! Have fun!!

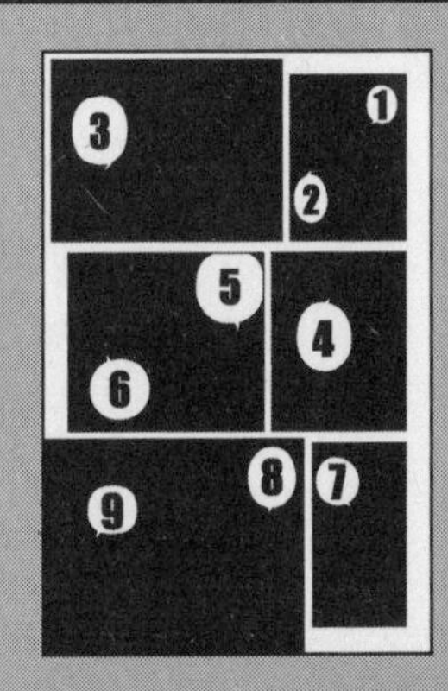

"Become You"

Lyrics and Arrangement by Kentarou Kobuchi
Performed by Kobukuro

You want to grow up as fast as you can, but right now life only seems to weigh you down
You cannot fast forward or rewind time, you're living life as it unfolds
You can't erase today's mistakes, only add to who you are each and every day
Only when you grow up, do you realize just how very high up the sky is.

For right now it's okay to not win. This is the time when you need to learn to fail
For right now it's okay not to get it. All these bitter feelings that you can't digest
For right now it's okay to be unable, for some things only come to us when we struggle
For right now it's okay to be lost, as long as you can proudly say you chose this path yourself

For right now it's okay not to meet, for our feelings will only grow stronger in the time we are apart
For right now it's okay that you can't see, for these feelings are greater than anything we can see
For right now it's okay to feel lonely, for there are so many you don't know who feel the same as you
For right now it's okay to be where you are, so you can decide where you go next on your own
For right now it's okay to be nothing. If you're empty then may you become genuine
For right now it's okay to remain as you are, so long as you can grow and change while holding on to that which you wish to keep

It is not you who can decide that you aren't wonderful or worthy,
For the ones who love you can see the you that awaits in the distant future

No matter if you screw up, or if you shine, they believe in you just the same
That love is the real thing, and so someday you will become the real you

For right now it's okay to not win, not to get it, to be unable
Okay to be lost, not to meet, that you can't say it, and to be lonely
For right now it's okay to stay put, to be nothing, to be just as you are
Because someday you will become the real you
Become the real you, become the real you

AFTERWORD

*"Kimi ni Nare" translates to "Become You."

BECOME THE REAL YOU.

RIGHT NOW...
NO MATTER HOW PAINFUL, HOW HARD, HOW DIFFICULT...
SOME-DAY...

SOME-DAY...

SOME-DAY...
YOU CAN...

Hikari...?
Someday, I'll...
Wait...
in the future...
RIGHT NOW...
I WOULD BE HAPPY TO REACH EVEN ONE PERSON.

In that case...
I'll be there for you.

Even if it doesn't come true...
I won't cast my dream aside!
AND I HAVEN'T.
EVEN NOW...
I CHERISH IT.

EVEN IF NOTHING COMES OF IT, IT'S NOT OVER.
I'VE FOUND SOMETHING I CAN DO.
Saving everyone in the world...
is, quite frankly, impossible.
There's just too much working against you.
Still...
I don't want to give up.

PLEASE LET ME SEE.
OKAY.
I'LL PROBABLY PAINT AGAIN SOMEDAY...
BECAUSE I REALLY DO LOVE IT.
Can I hug you?
NO.
EVEN IF THINGS DON'T GO WELL...
I'LL NEVER DENY MY DREAMS.

I LIKED YOUR PAINTING...
BETTER THAN ANY OF THE OTHERS.
IT WAS OF THE PENGUINS AT THE ZOO.
IT WAS BEAUTIFUL.
IF...
YOU STILL LIKE PAINT-ING...
AND YOU EVER PAINT AGAIN...

I SAW A PAINTING BY A MEMBER OF THE ART CLUB AT THE CULTURAL FESTIVAL.
I'VE NEVER BEEN ABLE TO FORGET IT.
THE FOLLOWING YEAR, I SEARCHED FOR MORE WORK FROM THAT ARTIST.
BUT HE HAD NOTHING ON DISPLAY.
WHEN I ASKED...
I WAS TOLD HE HAD QUIT THE ART CLUB.
IT WAS YOU.

EVEN IF YOU CAN'T PAINT WELL...
YOU STILL LIKE IT, DON'T YOU?
......
I ANSWERED YOUR QUESTION, REMEMBER?
IN MY SECOND YEAR OF JUNIOR HIGH...

I COULD HAVE BEEN THE VERSION OF ME...
SAKURA NEEDED.
HERE, HIKARI.
AS THANKS FOR PERFORMING WITH ME.
LEMON
Sparkling
Vitamin C 1500mg
Citric Acid 3000mg
CHEAP.
GIVE ME A BREAK!
I ONLY HAD 500 YEN ON ME TONIGHT!
WHAT ELSE IS NEW?
THANKS FOR TONIGHT!
YOU MADE ONE OF MY DREAMS COME TRUE.
YOU...
AREN'T GONNA PAINT ANYMORE?

WHENEVER I SEE YOU GIVING SOMETHING YOUR ALL, IT GIVES ME STRENGTH, TOO!
HEY, TAIYOU.
WHAT?
THERE'S BEEN SOMETHING I'VE BEEN MEANING TO TELL YOU... CAN WE TALK SOMETIME SOON?
HUH?
SURE! WE CAN TALK RIGHT NOW!
MAYBE NEXT TIME!
I WISH...

THANKS TO HIM, THE OUTSIDE WORLD NO LONGER SCARES ME.
TAIYOU!
Sakura!! I did it!
Yeah! Good job!
It wasn't perfect, but I'm getting better!
You were great!
No matter what any-one says, no one can drag me down!!
Totally!
SAKURA?
YOU WERE CRYING. YOU OKAY?
I WAS MOVED TO TEARS.

YOUR TEMPO WAS SLOW AS ALWAYS, BUT IN THE END WE SYNCED UP.
TODAY, YOU USED THE PIANO AS YOUR METRONOME, TAIYOU-KUN!
IT'S LIKE THE PIANO...
WAS GUIDING YOUR HANDS.
IT'S BECAUSE YOU PRACTICED SO HARD THAT YOU COULD FOLLOW ME WITHOUT FALLING BEHIND.
YOU'RE GETTING BETTER.
HIKARI WAS THE ONE WHO HELPED ME...
GET OUTSIDE OF MY OWN HEAD.

YOU WERE PERFECT.
IS IT JUST THE LEFT HAND THAT CAN'T MOVE? WHAT ABOUT THE RIGHT?
MY RIGHT HAND WORKS.
THE ONLY PROBLEMS ARE THE MIDDLE, RING, AND PINKY FINGERS.
THE TEMPO WAS SLOW ON OUR SONG TONIGHT, SO IT WAS JUST LITTLE THINGS.
UMM, WAS TODAY...
REALLY THE FIRST TIME YOU TWO PLAYED TOGETHER?
EVEN YOUR BREATHING WAS IN SYNC.
THAT'S BECAUSE HIKARI MATCHED UP WITH ME.
HE'S THE REASON IT WENT SO WELL.
IT'S NOT SOMETHING I COULD HAVE DONE ON MY OWN.

Hikari!!
Thank yoooou~!!!
That was incred-ible!!
SO MOVING!!
WHY ARE YOU DOING THAT WITH YOUR ARMS?
FOR A HUG!!
NO WAY.
I'M NORMALLY BETTER THAN THAT.

BUT IN THE END...
HE TOLD ME...
THAT IT WAS A BIG STEP.
A VERY BIG STEP.

HE MIGHT HAVE BEEN...
THE ONLY PERSON THERE NOT SMILING.

CLAP パチ
CLAP パチ
CLAP パチ
CLAP パチ
CLAP パチ
CLAP パチ
CLAP パチ
CLAP パチ
パチ CLAP
CLAP パチ
CLAP パチ
パチ CLAP
CLAP パチ
パチ CLAP
CLAP パチ
パチ CLAP
THANK YOU VERY MUCH!!

HE PLAYED THE PIANO...
AS IF IN A GREAT DEAL OF PAIN THAT DAY.
PHEW...
パチ
CLAP
CLAP
パチ

HIKARI REALLY IS AMAZING.
I'VE GOT NOTHING ON HIM.
THIS GUY HAS THE ABILITY TO IMPACT OTHERS.

IT'S ALL RIGHT.
SEE?

I WISH ALL THE PAIN COULD DISAPPEAR FROM THIS WORLD.
BUT WITHOUT PAIN...
PEOPLE CAN'T RECOG- NIZE...
KINDNESS.

MY CHEST STARTED BURNING.
SO MANY THINGS FLASHED THROUGH MY MIND.
I TRIED TO HOLD THEM BACK, BUT TEARS FLOWED DOWN MY FACE.
TO ME, HIKARI WAS LIKE AN ANGEL...
GUIDING ME THROUGH THE DARK-NESS.

I DIDN'T SAY ANYTHING BECAUSE I THOUGHT HE'D GET MAD.
I HEARD HIKARI PERFORM...
AT OUR JUNIOR HIGH'S COMPETITIONS IN OUR FIRST AND SECOND YEAR.
BUT THE PERFORMANCE THAT REALLY MOVED ME...
WAS DURING THIRD YEAR.
I HAD JUST QUIT ART CLUB.
I WASN'T SURE MYSELF WHY IT AFFECTED ME SO.

Our perfor-mance...
won't be flawless.
But we...
love music.
Things may not go perfectly...
but I promise...
we're going to give you our all.
CLAP
パチ
CLAP
パチ
CLAP
パチ

I WANTED TO SEE WHAT WE WOULD BE LIKE TOGETHER, EVEN JUST ONCE...
I want to get a few words in before we start.
I'll be playing the piano.
I'm sorry to start things off on a sour note, but...
my left hand...
is a bit messed up right now.
And he sucks at the guitar.

CRAP.
THIS IS BAD.
I'LL DO THE LEAD-IN.
START PLAYING AT MY SIGNAL.
OKAY.
I'M THE ONE WHO ASKED HIM, BUT NOW...
YOU NERVOUS?
HUH?
AH!
A-A LITTLE.
ME TOO.

TRACK5
Ashie
Taiyou

I FEEL LIKE THE TWO OF US CAN DO IT.
WE CAN CONQUER THE WORLD.
TOGETH-ER...

OKAY.
I CAN'T SURPASS HIKARI.
HIKARI HAS SOME-THING THAT, NO MATTER HOW HARD I TRY...
I NEVER WILL.
BUT THAT'S OKAY.
WHAT I CAN'T ACCOMPLISH ON MY OWN...

DON'T JUST STAND THERE!
I'M PLAYING THE PIANO.
YOU'RE GONNA PLAY THE *PIANO*?!
I KNOW WHAT SONG YOU'RE GONNA PLAY.
IT'S THE SAME ONE YOU ALWAYS PRACTICED IN THE PARK.
YEAH, THAT'S RIGHT!
PLAY LIKE YOU USUALLY DO.
LEAVE THE REST TO ME.

WAIT!
THAT ISN'T HIS LEFT HAND!
IT'S HIS RIGHT!
"If you wanna perform with me...
"raise your right hand."
NO WAY!!
Uh! Uhm...
this next song will be my last song!
With me will be my fr--
uh, my classmate, Tsukimoto Hikari-kun!
CLAP パチ
パチ CLAP
パチ CLAP

MY FIRST STEP.
HIKARI!!
DID YOU SEE ME?!
I did it!
!
"If you're enjoying it, raise your left hand."
I'M SO GLAD...

CLAP
CLAP
CLAP
CLAP
CLAP
CLAP
CLAP
THIS IS...

ONE ...
BY ONE ...
THEY'RE GETTING INTO IT.
IT'S MAKING THEM...
SMILE.
THIS IS SO MUCH FUN!!

THEY...
LIKE IT?

Stop letting other people control you.
Believe in yourself.
You've worked so hard.
BEING POSITIVE...
TAKES A LOT OF COURAGE.
Chin up.
The world is up here.

Right now, you are your own worst enemy.
You're still afraid.
Too scared to make a move.
You're afraid your efforts...
will just get torn apart by other people.
You're afraid you'll be told...
that your dreams are worth-less or impossible.
That you'll never live up to their standards.

SO MUCH FARTHER.
TODAY...
I WANT TO MAKE YOU ALL SMILE.
This is my first step.
Can you really do this alone?
I can. I've got this guitar.
Even if you can change other people's hearts through music...
you can't change your own.

NO, I CAN DO THIS.
EVERY DAY...
EVERY SINGLE DAY...
I'VE PLAYED MY HEART OUT.
I'VE BEEN WORKING SO HARD FOR TODAY.
BUT I WAS NEVER ALONE.
I HAD HIKARI.
SINCE I MET HIM...
I'VE BEEN ABLE TO REACH...

TWANG
TEMPO.
RHYTHM.
I GET IT.
MAYBE IT IS IMPOSSIBLE.
BUT NO MATTER WHAT, MY FINGERS CAN'T KEEP UP.

ASHIE-KUN, GET READY!
OKAY!
I WANNA CHEER SAKURA UP, TOO.
I'LL HAVE TO FIGURE SOMETHING OUT.
I'm Ashie Taiyou.
I'm a third year in high school. My dream is to be a musician.
I SOUNDED PRETTY GOOD JUST NOW.
I WONDER...
HOW HIKARI KNEW ABOUT ME AND THE ART CLUB.
UGH, NOW'S NOT THE TIME FOR THAT. CALM DOWN, TAIYOU!
HAAAH...

THEN...
EVERYONE WOULD BE ABLE TO SMILE.
HIKARI.
I'M GONNA KEEP MY CHIN UP.
SO!
IF YOU'RE ENJOYING IT, RAISE YOUR LEFT HAND!
JUST DROP THIS HAND BIT ALREADY.

EVERYONE HAS THOSE FEELINGS DEEP DOWN INSIDE.
AND EVERYONE HAS THE POWER TO OVERCOME THEM.
I WISH I COULD ERASE ALL THE HARDSHIPS FROM THIS WORLD.

WHAT ARE YOU PLAYING?
THE SONG I DID AT THE FESTIVAL, PLUS ONE MORE.
EVEN IF YOU MESS UP, IT'S OKAY.
I WON'T!
IF YOU WANNA PERFORM WITH ME, JUST RAISE YOUR RIGHT HAND.
STOP TALKING LIKE A DENTIST!
WHEN I QUIT DRAWING...
I WAS SO DEPRESSED.
WHY WAS IT JUST ME...
WHO FELT THIS WAY?
BUT...
IT WASN'T JUST ME.
EVERYONE EXPERIENCES HARDSHIPS.

HE'S GONNA BE IN A COMPETITION SOON...
SO HE WANTED TO PRACTICE.
THAT'S WHY HE'S ALL DRESSED UP TODAY!
So cute!
I WANNA HEAR YOU PERFORM, HIKARI.
I WANT THESE PEOPLE TO HEAR YOU.
AND...
I WANT IT TO BRING THEM JOY.
LIKE IT DID FOR ME.

THE PERSON I AM NOW...
COULD NEVER PAINT THOSE PICTURES.
TAKE IT OFF!
HIKARI, YOU HAVE NO SENSE OF FASHION!
IT LOOKS GOOD!
YEAH! IT LOOKS GREAT, SENPAI!
You're a true artist!
You guys have no sense at all.
YOU LOOK LIKE AN ACORN AT A SPELLING BEE.
ACORN?!
AN ACORN AT A SPELLING BEE?! MANAKA?!
THAT'S SO MEAN! SURE, HE LOOKS LIKE A NERD, BUT AN ACORN?! REALLY?!
You're the one going on and on about him being an acorn. How mean!
MANAKA-KUN, YOU'RE UP!
YES, SIR!
HUH?

It's because you were alone.
There was no one who appreciated you or your art.
Humans need that support...
to keep going.
Even just the slightest taste.
THE WORLD OUTSIDE IS HARSH AND PAINFUL.
IT'S NOT ALL PRETTY PICTURES, ON AND ON FOREVER.
I LEARNED THAT FROM MY ART TEACHER.

I SUCK AT THE GUITAR...
I STILL LOVE MUSIC.
So you think something can still be worthwhile even if the world's against you?
Then why...
did you quit painting?

CAN I JUST ASK YOU ONE THING?
I KNOW YOU HATE PLAYING PIANO, HIKARI,
BUT YOU STILL LIKE MUSIC, DON'T YOU?
I DO!
Not you, Manaka!
EVEN IF...

TWANG
YOU'RE SO ANNOYING.
WHY ARE YOU PRACTICING *HERE*?
GO PRACTICE IN THAT CLOSET BY YOURSELF!
BUT IF I GO IN THERE, YOU'LL GET MAD AT ME.
I'LL ALLOW IT. GO.
THANK YOU!
I wasn't talking to you.
I HAVE NO BUSINESS TEACHING YOU THE GUITAR.
AND NO MATTER HOW MANY TIMES YOU ASK, I'M NOT PERFORMING WITH YOU.

I'VE HEARD THAT ARTISTIC TYPES ARE MORE PRONE TO MENTAL ILLNESS.
I THINK THAT'S BECAUSE ...
THEY LIVE IN THEIR OWN WORLDS INSIDE THEIR HEADS.
THEIR WORLD AND THE OUTSIDE WORLD.
IDEAL VERSUS REALITY.
IT CAN MAKE ONE BELIEVE ONE HAS NO FRIENDS IN THE OUTSIDE WORLD.
♪
♬
♪

TRACK4
Ashie
Taiyou

NOW...

I WOULD HAVE THE STRENGTH...

TO ASK FOR HELP.

WHEN I WAS IN HIGH SCHOOL...
NO MATTER WHAT I DID...
I WAS LOST AND CONFUSED.
I'VE GROWN SO MUCH SINCE THEN. IF I COULD DO IT AGAIN...
I'D BE A SOURCE OF STRENGTH FOR SAKURA AND HIKARI.
I'D STAND UP TO THAT TEACHER.
BUT BACK THEN, I COULDN'T.
Have you found allies?
No.
I'll do it by myself.

WHY WERE YOU CRYING?
I TOLD YOU! BECAUSE OF MY SISTER'S TEXT!
SEE YA!
I'LL BE AT YOUR PERFORMANCE!
GIVE IT YOUR ALL!
BYE!

H-
HE'S MY BOYFRIEND NOW!
IT'S NONE OF YOUR BUSINESS, TAIYOU...
SO JUST DROP IT!
REALLY?
YEAH.
SO...
YOU'RE GOING OUT?
YES.

You're always cute, Sakura!
Stop, you're embarrass-ing me!
How can you say that with a straight face?!
WHY NOT? I ALWAYS SAY IT!
YOU'RE THE ONLY ONE...
WHO SAYS SO, TAIYOU.
WHAT ABOUT THE BOY YOU LIKE IN PHOTOGRAPHY CLUB?
NOT SO MUCH...
I SEE.
LET'S GO!
WHAT'S HIS NAME?!
NOT TELLING!
I WANNA SEE WHAT HE LOOKS LIKE! GOT A PICTURE?
NOPE!
THEN I'LL STOP BY THE PHOTO-GRAPHY CLUB AND SEE FOR MYSELF!

OH, THAT?
MY SISTER SENT ME THIS TEXT MESSAGE.
I MADE HER LUNCH TODAY..
AND SHE ACTUALLY SAID THANK YOU.
Tsubomi
Lunch was delicious.
Thank you. ♡
Just finished club so I'm heading home.
I WAS CRYING BECAUSE I WAS HAPPY.
HUH? REALLY? THAT'S ALL?
YUP.
REALLY?
YEAH!
IT'S THE FIRST TIME SHE'S EVER SAID THAT.
YOU'RE ADORABLE, SAKURA.

SAKURA!!
WHAT'S WRONG?!
DID SOMETHING HAPPEN?!
NOTHING HAPPENED!
You surprised me!
THEN WHY WERE YOU WERE CRYING?!
HUH?
PFFT!
AH HA HA!

I'M SORRY I SAID...
YOU HAD NO TALENT.
BA-CHAK...
HIKARI PRAISED ME...
EVEN THOUGH I HAVEN'T ACHIEVED ANYTHING.
IF I DIDN'T HAVE HIKARI...
I HAVE NO IDEA WHAT I WOULD HAVE DONE.

I REALLY...
CAN'T HELP YOU.
I'M AS BAD AS THAT TEACHER.
I MOCKED YOU.
NO.
I CAN'T...
HELP YOU PRACTICE ANYMORE, EITHER.
I'M SORRY.
HIKARI ...
PRAISED ME.

BUT...
IT DIDN'T WORK OUT.
IT'S SO FRUSTRAT-ING.
HIKARI.
I WANNA PERFORM WITH YOU...
NO MATTER WHAT.
I DON'T GET WHY YOU'RE SO OBSESSED WITH IT BEING ME.

I HAD GRABBED THE KNIFE WITH MY DOMINANT HAND.
BUT IT DIDN'T AFFECT MY ABILITY TO DRAW.
WHEN I PLAY GUITAR...
MY FINGERS SOMETIMES CRAMP UP, BUT IT'S NOT A BIG DEAL.
THE REASON I CAN'T REALLY PLAY IS BECAUSE I'M BAD AT IT.
BUT I THOUGHT THAT IF I KEPT AT IT, SOMETHING GOOD WOULD COME OF IT.
LIKE I COULD OVER-COME...
MY PAST DISAPPOINT-MENTS BY FINDING SUCCESS ELSEWHERE.

They're *my* pictures!
Even if they're ugly...
even if no one wants or needs them...
they still matter to *me*.

Crossing your work out will only improve it.
SHWIK
WHAP
Stop!!
Let go!
Hey!

CLATTER
I hate punks like you more than anything!
You think you can just do whatever you want!
Moriya actually *does* what I tell him!
You can't hack it, but you wanna run your mouth!
There are loads of people better than you!
You have *zero* talent!

What are you doing?
I thought you'd left.
I was just about to check your picture.
So the one putting the "X" on my pictures was *you*, Sensei?
That's right.
I needed to find some way to get through to you.
But...
you don't have to ruin my pictures!
I'm not "ruining" anything. Work like this belongs in the trash!
YANK
It's not trash!!

Good-bye.
Bye.
Ah!
Crap! I forgot something.
You go on ahead!
BUT I ALREADY KNEW...
WHO WAS DOING IT.

SOMEONE HAD CROSSED OUT THE POND PICTURE.
ALL MY HARD WORK RUINED, MARKED UP BY RED PEN.
Who...?
BUT THE NEXT DAY...
AND THE DAY AFTER THAT...
Sensei?
I'm gonna go paint outside again today.
Be back by five.
Okay.
AND EVEN THE DAY AFTER THAT...
THE RED X SHOWED UP AGAIN AND AGAIN.
There's no way it was Moriya.

BUT...
MAYBE I CAN HELP YOU.
TRY TELLING ME ABOUT IT.
I'VE NEVER TOLD ANYONE THE WHOLE STORY...
BECAUSE ...
I KNEW IT WAS MY FAULT.

IS THAT TRUE?
IT'S WHAT I TOLD HER.
I'VE NEVER TOLD ANYONE WHAT REALLY HAPPENED.
TELL ME.
IF I DO...
WILL YOU PERFORM WITH ME?
HEY, *I* WON THE BET.
AND THAT WASN'T THE DEAL.

I WONDER IF THE REASON...
YOU'RE NOT GETTING BETTER, NO MATTER HOW MUCH YOU PRACTICE...
IS BECAUSE OF YOUR HAND?
SORRY.
I ASKED HER ABOUT IT DURING THE CULTURAL FESTIVAL.
SAKURA?
SHE SAID IT WAS AN ACCIDENT THAT HAPPENED IN ART CLUB.

THAT'S MY SECRET!
NOW YOU KNOW WHY I QUIT THE ART CLUB!
Okay, practice time!!
I've been getting better at hearing my heart metro-nome!
I still don't get it, though.
WAIT.
YOU STILL HAVEN'T TOLD ME EVERY-THING.
YEAH, I HAVE.
GRAB
SHOW ME...
YOUR LEFT HAND.

I DIDN'T WANNA GIVE UP...
BUT NO MATTER HOW I TRIED, I COULDN'T DRAW ANYMORE. SO, IN MY THIRD YEAR OF JUNIOR HIGH, I QUIT THE ART CLUB.
IT WAS HARD.
I HAD NOTHING LEFT.
BUT THEN I SAW...
YOU AND YOUR PIANO!
I HEARD YOU PLAY ACCOMPANIMENT DURING THE CHORUS COMPETITION.
IT SAVED ME.
I THOUGHT I'D LIKE TO TRY MAKING MUSIC, TOO.

I HAD NO IDEA WHAT I SHOULD DO.
WHAT COULD I HAVE DRAWN TO GAIN HIS PRAISE?
WHAT WAS WRONG, WHAT WAS RIGHT?
NO MATTER HOW HARD I TRIED...
HE WOULD NEVER RECOGNIZE MY ABILITIES IF I DIDN'T TOE THE LINE.
IN THE END...
I REALIZED HOW VITAL NATURAL TALENT WAS.

MY PICTURE THAT I CHERISHED SO MUCH.
I COULDN'T DRAW ANYMORE.
WHEN-EVER I TRIED...
THAT VOICE WOULD ECHO IN MY MIND.
"That's not the right color.
"Look at his picture."
Nnn...

Come on.
When are you going to grow up?
Draw it again.
Do it till you get it right.
BUT...
THE COLOR DIDN'T SEEM "WRONG" TO ME.
I JUST...
WANTED TO PAINT SOMETHING PRETTY.
IT WAS *MY* PICTURE.

St-
stop!
ガシャッ
KRSH
SPLUSH

But this color's better.
The pond is duller than that.
We stop using bright blue for lakes and ponds in elementary school.
But... this color is prettier.
But your paintings aren't realistic.
I'm fine with that.
SIGH...
Why can't you be like Moriya and paint *correctly*?
Let me see that.
CLATTER...
!

Moriya painted it better.
Go take a look.
Okay.
Moriya, lemme see!
Wow, that's really good!
MY PAINTING WAS DIFFERENT FROM THE WALL'S REAL COLOR...
BUT STILL, IT ENDED UP LOOKING REALLY NEAT.
IT WAS GREY WITH A DASH OF PURPLE.
I WANTED TO USE THAT COLOR.
WHEN I FOLLOWED THE INSTRUCTIONS GIVEN, MY PICTURE LOOKED BETTER.
BUT IT WASN'T THE PICTURE I HAD WANTED TO PAINT.
Ashie...
is that the right color for the pond?

I LEARNED HOW FROM A SHOW ON TV.
I LOVED IT SO MUCH, I DID IT ALL THE TIME.
I KNEW THE ONLY WAY TO GET BETTER WAS TO KEEP PRACTICING.
Ashie.
Is that *really* the color of that wall?
I... I should have made it more beige...
No, sir...

WHY DID YOU QUIT ART CLUB?
THERE'S MORE TO THE STORY.
TELL ME WHAT HAPPENED.
I'VE ALWAYS WANTED TO KNOW.
WHEN I WAS A LITTLE KID, I FELL IN LOVE WITH PAINTING.

POINT, TSUKI-MOTO-KUN!
TSUKI-MOTO-KUN WINS!!
NOOOO !!
WOOOOW!
AMAZING!
WHY DID YOU GO SO HARD ALL OF A SUDDEN?!
I've never seen Tsuki-moto move like that before!
HE CAN REALLY JUMP!
I'M NOT EVEN WORRIED ABOUT THE WAGER--THAT WAS JUST ROUGH!
WINNING ISN'T EVERY-THING.
NOW YOU KNOW THE TRUE WEIGHT OF LOSING.
YOU DON'T HAVE TO RUB IT IN!
SO?
WHAT DO I HAVE TO DO?

I'M NOT GONNA LOSE!
I WILL...
GET HIKARI TO PERFORM WITH ME!
THWAP
ス
ROLL...
HUFF
HUFF
HUFF

NO, YOU'RE NOT!
YOU AREN'T EVEN TRYING!
YOU'RE NOT EVEN MOVING AROUND!
I DON'T HAVE TO MOVE, I JUST HAVE TO WAIT FOR IT TO FLY OVER.
BUT YOU'RE NOT SENDING IT BACK!
MAYBE HE'S GOT BAD REFLEXES?!
HOW ABOUT A BET?!
FIRST ONE TO TWENTY-ONE POINTS WINS.
IF YOU LOSE, YOU HAVE TO PLAY WITH ME IN MY NEXT SHOW.
AND IF YOU LOSE?
I'll give you ten umaibo sticks!
That's no prize.
No thanks!
LET'S SEE...
IF YOU LOSE...
YOU HAVE TO DO ONE THING I TELL YOU, NO MATTER WHAT.
NOW THAT'S UNFAIR!
It could be anything!
BUT FINE!

"Save the world"?
You won't be able to do it alone.
You need allies.
ズバッ
THWACK
HIKARI!!
ARE YOU TAKING THIS SERIOUSLY?!
I AM.

B
D
H
I
A
A
TRACK3
Ashie
Taiyou

That's right... every single person.
Everyone.
I WILL...
MAKE UP FOR MY PAST MISTAKES.

SO IT'S NOT LIKE JUST ANYONE WILL DO.
Save the world?
That's why you wanna play music?
I don't wanna see people fighting or in pain...
or suffering or crying.
I wanna make everyone everywhere smile.
And through music, I can.
Everyone every-where?

I KNOW HE'S GOT ISSUES.

BUT THE ONE WHO SHOWED ME MY DREAMS WERE POSSIBLE...
THAT YOU REALLY COULD CHANGE PEOPLE'S HEARTS THROUGH MUSIC...
WAS HIKARI.

After that, senpai no longer played in competitions.
I heard he even quit taking lessons.
No one knows why.
"My fingers are a bit stiff."

Last year, at the prefectural piano competition...
Tsukimoto-senpai was scheduled to perform as usual...
but apparently, he was acting strange.
They say...
from the moment he took the stage, the song was off and he made numerous mistakes.
It was like he was a totally different person.
And then he just...
stopped playing, right in the middle of the song...
and started crying.

Tsukimoto-senpai is a prodigy!
He's played piano from a very young age, been in lots of music competitions, and won tons of awards.
People throw around the word "genius" a lot, but Tsukimoto-kun actually deserves it.
But I think it would be really hard to get him...
to perform in the cultural festival, don't you?
Why?
It's just a rumor I heard, so I don't know the details...

HIKARI IS TRYING TO PUSH AWAY HIS PAST, TOO.
I'LL TRY...
TO GIVE HIM MORE SPACE.
Manaka-kun!
How are you?
Ashie-senpai!
I already told you I wasn't joining your club!
GYAAHH!
I'm gonna be kidnapped!!
No, that's not it!
Manaka-kun, you're learning piano, right?
Do you know Tsukimoto Hikari-kun?
Yeah, of course!
What do you know about him?

I ALWAYS HATED THE PIANO, SO I QUIT.

THAT'S ALL.

DO YOUR BEST...

AT THIS CAFÉ.

I'LL BE CHEERING YOU ON.

I HAVE SECRETS, TOO.

I STARTED PLAYING MUSIC BECAUSE I WAS RUNNING AWAY FROM SOMETHING.

I KEPT IT A SECRET AND HOPED IT WOULD GO AWAY.

IN JUNIOR HIGH...
YOU WERE IN THE ART CLUB, WEREN'T YOU?
HOW...
DOES HE KNOW THAT?
I...
STARTED TO HATE DRAWING AND PAINTING, SO I QUIT.
THAT'S ALL...
I SEE.
WELL, THE REASON I QUIT PIANO HAS NOTHING TO DO WITH MY HANDS.

YOU DIDN'T TELL ME YOU WERE GOING TO A MUSIC SCHOOL IN TOKYO.
HUH?! DID YOU WANNA GO WITH ME?
THAT'S NOT IT!
WHEN YOU SAID, "LET'S FORM A BAND," WAS IT JUST A WHIM?
JUST SOMETHING TO KILL TIME BEFORE COLLEGE?
THAT'S NOT IT!
I MEAN... YOU NEVER OPEN UP TO ME, HIKARI.
I CAN NEVER TELL WHAT YOU'RE THINKING!
"OPEN UP"?
HOW ABOUT YOU GO FIRST, THEN?
WHY DID YOU JOIN THE MODERN MUSIC CLUB?

YESS!!
WE GOT A PERFORMANCE SPACE!!
LET'S PERFORM TOGETHER, HIKARI!
......
I TOLD YOU NO.
YOU CAN DO ANYTHING YOU WANT!
EVEN JUST STAND NEXT TO ME!
No.
And what would people say about a guy just standing there?
WHY DON'T YOU ASK THAT FRIEND OF YOURS?
I'M SURE ACORN BOY WILL SAY YES.
IT DOESN'T HAVE TO BE ME, RIGHT?
WHAT ARE YOU GETTING SO MAD ABOUT?

HERE'S OUR STAGE.
YOU CAN PERFORM HERE SATURDAYS AND SUNDAYS WHILE OUR CUSTOMERS EAT AND CHAT.
EVEN I CAN PERFORM HERE?!
SURE, IF YOU SIGN UP.
YOU CAN ONLY PERFORM AFTER SIX ON SATURDAY AND SUNDAY EVENINGS.
YOU'RE A GUITAR-IST?
Yes, sir!
WE'RE PRETTY FLEXIBLE, SO JUST PLAY WHATEVER YOU WANT.
What-ever I want?!
UMM...
I STILL KINDA SUCK, IS THAT OKAY?!
AH HA HA!
OF COURSE! BEGINNERS ARE TOTALLY WELCOME!

AH, YEAH. I'M ON MY WAY TO MEET HIM.
HUH?
Wha? Huh?
WELL, GOOD LUCK!
SAKURA...
SEEMED KINDA DOWN.
SHE SEEMED LIKE HER USUAL SELF TO ME. ?
NO, I'VE KNOWN HER FOR A LONG TIME.
SOMETHING WAS UP.
MAYBE SHE'S HAVING ISSUES WITH THAT GUY SHE LIKES.
......
YOU REALLY ARE AN IDIOT.
I'M SERIOUS!
LET'S GO.

SO, I HAD NO CHOICE...
BUT TO BE SNEAKY ABOUT IT.
WHAT IS THIS PLACE?
IT'S A CAFÉ WHERE YOU COULD PERFORM!
I CAN PERFORM IN A CAFÉ?
YEAH! A FRIEND TOLD ME ABOUT IT!
YOU STILL NEED TO ASK THE STAFF, THOUGH.
WELL, I HAVE STUFF TO DO, SO I'M OFF.
AHH...
UM...
HOW ABOUT THAT GUY YOU LIKE? ARE THINGS GOING WELL?

I'VE SEEN YOU PLAY...
AT THE CHORUS CONCERT.
HOW COME YOU DON'T PLAY ANY--
I HAVE NOTHING TO SAY TO YOU.
IF YOU'RE GONNA BRING THAT UP, THEN GET OUT.
S-SORRY.
TALKING ABOUT THE PIANO OR HIS HANDS...
MADE HIM ANGRY.
HE WOULDN'T TELL ME ANYTHING.

I'VE NEVER SEEN YOU LAUGH OR SMILE.
YOU *CAN* SMILE, RIGHT?
THERE ARE THINGS I ENJOY.
IT JUST DOESN'T SHOW IT ON MY FACE.
AND YOUR BIT ABOUT THE DENTIST WASN'T FUNNY.
OKAY! WHEN YOU'RE FEELING HAPPY, SHOW ME BY HOLDING UP YOUR LEFT HAND!
OKAY, *NOW* YOU SOUND LIKE A DENTIST!
TSUKIMOTO-SENPAI?
YOU DON'T PLAY THE PIANO ANYMORE?
MANAKA!
I'M LEARNING TO PLAY THE PIANO, TOO!
EVERYONE KNOWS ABOUT YOUR SKILLS, TSUKIMOTO-SENPAI!
YOU'RE FAMOUS!
A GENIUS!

IT'S NOT LIKE I WANNA BE WORLD RENOWNED OR ANY-THING.
I JUST HATE TO SEE PEOPLE SUFFERING OR SAD.
I WANNA CREATE A WORLD WHERE EVERYONE CAN SMILE.
ER...
HIKARI, IS THERE ANYTHING YOU ENJOY?
HUH?
Saying I wanna make the world smile...
makes me sound more like a comedian or a dentist than a musician!
Or some-thing...
AH HA HA HA!
WHY THOSE THREE CHOICES?
Dentist? That's funny!
AND YOU, A COMEDIAN? THAT'S A GOOD ONE!

HAVE YOU PICKED YOUR CAREER PATH?
NOPE.
HAVE YOU?
SORT OF.
YOU'RE GOING TO A MUSIC SCHOOL IN TOKYO, RIGHT?
NOPE.
TAIYOU-KUN'S DREAM IS TO BE A MUSICIAN!
HMPH.
YOU SAY "MUSICIAN," BUT IT'S NOT THAT SIMPLE.
WHY DO YOU WANNA PLAY MUSIC?
TO BE FAMOUS.
I WASN'T ASKING YOU.
YOU'LL LAUGH...
JUST TELL ME.
I WANNA... CHANGE THE WORLD.

THE MUSIC VENUE'S RATING FELL *AGAIN!*

Whatever.

RATINGS ASIDE, ISN'T THERE ANYWHERE ELSE YOU CAN PERFORM?

NO.

THAT'S RIGHT. THIS TOWN ONLY HAS TWO MUSIC VENUES.

YOU COULD ALWAYS DO A STREET PERFORMANCE.

Though the space in front of the train station is off-limits.

......

AND WHO ARE *YOU?*

OH, HE AND I RECENTLY BECAME FRIENDS.

I'M MANAKA, A SECOND-YEAR.

THANK YOU SO MUCH FOR INVITING ME HERE TODAY!

I DIDN'T INVITE YOU.

BY THE WAY, DON'T YOU ALL HAVE ENTRANCE EXAMS?

IS IT OKAY FOR YOU TO NOT BE STUDYING?

......

HEY, HIKARI...

DO YOU HAVE ANY DREAMS?

I HAD TO FACE MY WEAK-NESSES TO MOVE FORWARD.
"It's so frus-trating!"
AND THAT DAY...
I THINK I GREW A LITTLE STRONGER.
OH NO!!

THERE'S NOTHING TO BE GAINED BY LOOKING AT YOUR FEET.
MY SAVING GRACE...
IS THAT I STAY POSITIVE, NO MATTER WHAT.
BUT THAT'S PROB-ABLY...
BECAUSE I'M ONLY HALF AS GOOD AS MOST PEOPLE.
HIKARI.
I WANT TO DO ANOTHER CONCERT.
I WANT A SECOND SHOT!

MY PERFORMANCE WAS TERRIBLE.
THE AUDIENCE MUST HAVE BEEN SO BORED...
THAT'S NOT TRUE.
EVERYONE IS SMILING.
THEY LIKED IT!
YEAH.
EVEN IF YOU DO SUCK AT THE GUITAR.
MRR...
BUT YOU KNOW...
SEEING YOU TRY YOUR HARDEST IN SPITE OF EVERYTHING...
WAS VERY COOL.
SO CHEER UP.
THAT'S WHAT YOU'RE GOOD AT, AFTER ALL.

I BROUGHT THESE FOR YOU.
THEY'RE PHOTOS FROM THE CONCERT.
Whoa!!
I look so cool!!
Look, Hikari!
Isn't Sakura an amazing photogra-pher?!
HUH? WHAT'S WITH THAT FACE?!
SAKURA?! YOU TOO?!
THEY'RE NOT VERY GOOD, THOUGH.
WHAT?! THIS PICTURE'S AWESOME!
BUT YOU WERE LOOKING DOWN THE WHOLE TIME.
YOU DIDN'T LOOK AT THE CAMERA, EVEN ONCE.
THAT'S BECAUSE...
I COULDN'T BRING MYSELF TO LOOK OUT AT THE CROWD.

DID YOU ALWAYS PRACTICE LIKE THIS, HIKARI?
WHEN YOU PLAYED THE PIANO?
YOU'RE INCREDIBLE!
ANY REAL MUSICIAN PRACTICES THIS WAY.
KA-CHK
THERE YOU ARE!
SAKURA!
SORRY FOR INTERRUPTING YOUR PRACTICE.
HOW DID YOU FIND US?
I SPENT TWO YEARS FINDING THIS SPOT--
TAIYOU TOLD ME ABOUT IT.

TIC
TIC
Y-YOU DID GOOD JUST NOW.
TIC
BE MORE SPECIFIC!
UH, YOUR FINGERS ARE REALLY LONG.
TING
SAY IT WITH A BETTER TEMPO!
TIC
YOUR SINGING'S PRETTY GOOD.
TIC
MORE!
YOU'RE ONLY GOOD AT SINGING!
MORE!!
TIC
YOUR SINGING!
IT'S REALLY GOOD!!
TING
HUFF!
HUFF!
YOU JUST KEPT SAYING THE SAME THING OVER AND OVER. AND WHAT'S UP WITH SAYING MY FINGERS ARE LONG?
IS PLAYING WITH A METRONOME SUPPOSED TO BE THIS HARD?
And that "ting" noise is really annoying.
HUFF!
HEY, WHO'S THE TEACHER HERE?!
EVEN I'M FEELING DISCOUR-AGED.

TIC
THE METRONOME IN MY HEART...?
TIC
TIC
TING
GIVE IT A SHOT.
TIC
FIRST, SYNC UP WITH THE METRONOME.
TIC
TIC
TIC
UGH...
TIC
TING
THIS IS HARD.
YOU'RE SLIPPING!
KEEP UP!
TIC
TIC
HUH?
CAN'T YOU SAY SOMETHING NICE?!
TIC
TIC
DON'T BE SO MEAN!
I'M THE TYPE WHO DOES BETTER WHEN HE'S PRAISED!

HEY!
DON'T FALL ASLEEP!
ZZZ...
THE RHYTHM IN YOUR PERFORMANCE WAS CRAP!
THE TEMPO WAS AWFUL AND LISTENING TO YOU MADE ME *SICK*.
FROM NOW ON, USE THIS METRONOME WHEN YOU PRACTICE.
PLAY AT A COMFORT-ABLE, EVEN TEMPO!
FEEL THE RHYTHM IN YOUR *BONES!*
PRACTICE UNTIL YOU HEAR THE METRONOME IN YOUR *HEART!*

Why...
do you play music?
TNK
LISTEN.
TWO OF THE MOST IMPORTANT THINGS IN MUSIC ARE RHYTHM AND TEMPO.
RHYTHM AND TEMPO...
THAT'S NOT JUST TRUE FOR MUSIC.
IN MOVIES, NOVELS, MANGA, COMEDY...
EVEN SCHOOL REQUIRES BOTH.
OTHERWISE YOU MIGHT GET BORED AND DRIFT OFF.

TRACK2
Ashie
Taiyou

I STILL...

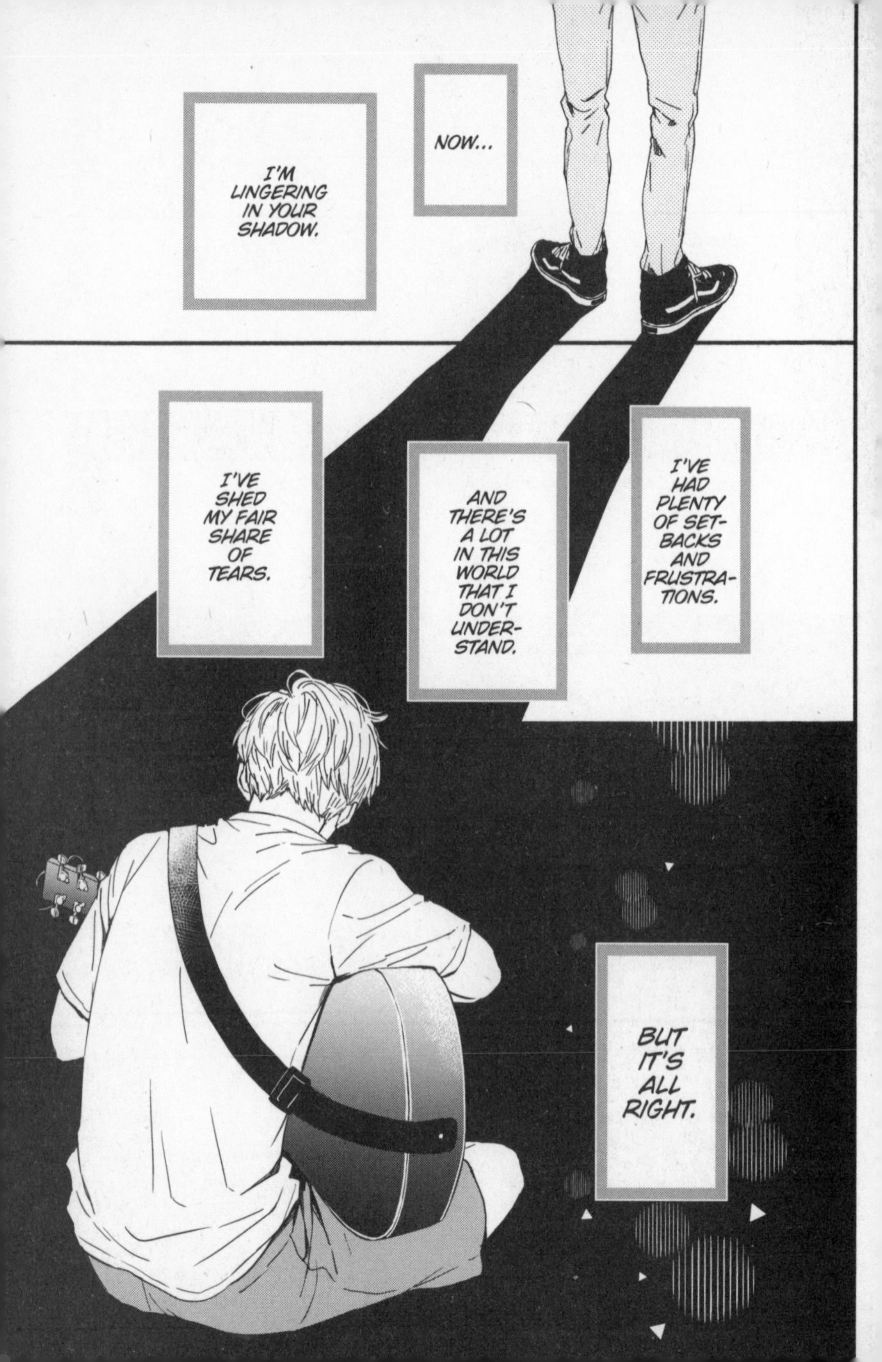
NOW...
I'M LINGERING IN YOUR SHADOW.
I'VE HAD PLENTY OF SET-BACKS AND FRUSTRA-TIONS.
AND THERE'S A LOT IN THIS WORLD THAT I DON'T UNDER-STAND.
I'VE SHED MY FAIR SHARE OF TEARS.
BUT IT'S ALL RIGHT.

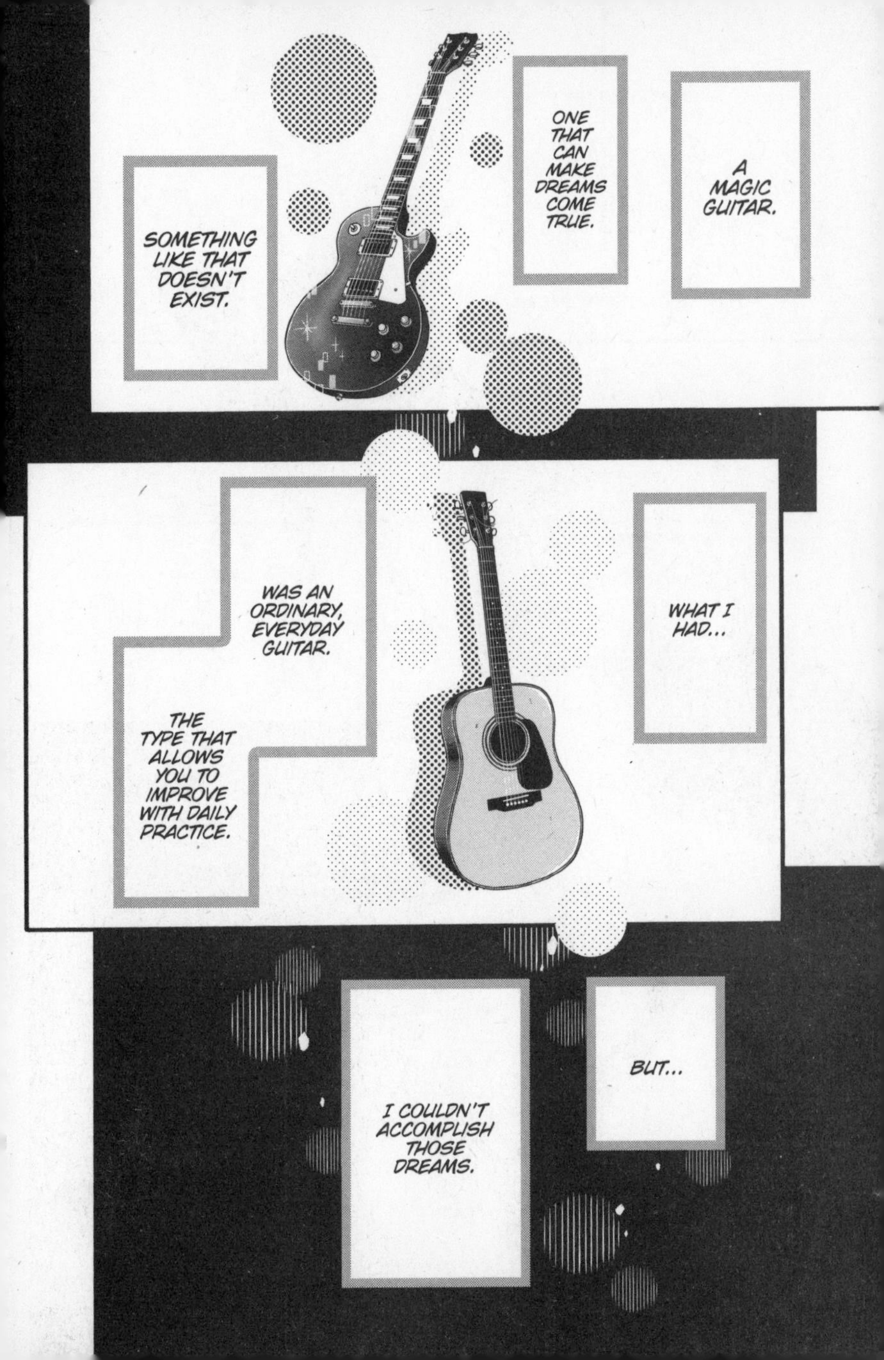
A MAGIC GUITAR.
ONE THAT CAN MAKE DREAMS COME TRUE.
SOMETHING LIKE THAT DOESN'T EXIST.
WHAT I HAD...
WAS AN ORDINARY, EVERYDAY GUITAR.
THE TYPE THAT ALLOWS YOU TO IMPROVE WITH DAILY PRACTICE.
BUT...
I COULDN'T ACCOMPLISH THOSE DREAMS.

BUT I CAN'T PLAY ANY INSTRU- MENTS.
I CAN ONLY TEACH YOU HOW TO PLAY.
OKAY!

Taiyou, you were so cool!
SAKURA ...
I'LL...
HELP YOU WITH YOUR STUPID BAND.

THERE ARE PLENTY OF CHUMPS WHO CAN PLAY WITH-OUT MUCH EFFORT.
BUT IF PERSEVERANCE IS A KIND OF TALENT...
THEN YOU HAVE LOTS OF TALENT.
I COULDN'T... DO WHAT YOU DO.
SO I THINK YOU'RE AMAZING.
PERSEVERANCE IS A TALENT...?
I'M NOT THE ONLY ONE...
WHO FEELS THAT WAY.

EVERY DAMN DAY I'VE HEARD YOU.
I KEEP THINKING YOU'LL SKIP A DAY...
BUT YOU'RE ALWAYS THERE, PRACTICING FOR HOURS LIKE A MADMAN.
WANT ANYONE TO SEE HOW HARD I WAS TRYING.
MY HOUSE IS RIGHT BESIDE...
THE PARK WHERE YOU PRACTICE.
I NEVER GET TO READ IN PEACE.
I THOUGHT IT WOULD LOOK COOLER IF I JUST HAD NATURAL TALENT.
I DIDN'T ...

IT'S SO FRUS-TRATING!
THAT SOUNDS SO PATHETIC.
YOU DIDN'T BOMB.
I'VE HEARD YOU PLAY.
AND NOT JUST TODAY, BUT ALL THE OTHER TIMES.

WHAT ARE YOU DOING HERE?
THIS IS MY SPOT.
HIKARI, I'M SORRY!
YOU PROBABLY SAW IT, BUT...
I BOMBED HARD.
I COULDN'T PLAY AT ALL LIKE I WANTED TO.
I WAS A MESS.
I ACTED LIKE I HAD IT ALL COVERED.
I SHOULD HAVE PRACTICED HARDER.
BUT NEXT TIME...
NEXT TIME, I'LL BE BETTER.
HIKARI...

THAT'S THE TRUTH.
THAT KID'S A WRECK.
I JUST THOUGHT...
I WAS CAPABLE OF **MORE.**
TSUKI-MOTO-KUN!
DO YOU KNOW WHERE TAIYOU WENT?
I WAS LOOKING FOR HIM, TOO.
HE'S NOT ANSWERING HIS PHONE OR MY TEXTS!
I HAVE AN IDEA OF WHERE HE MIGHT BE.
TSUKI-MOTO-KUN...
IF YOU FIND HIM, TELL HIM THIS FOR ME...

THIS IS MY REALITY.
I...
KNOW THE TRUTH.
I'M PA-THETIC.

MY FINGERS...
CAN'T KEEP UP!
I WANTED TO BELIEVE I HAD TALENT.
THAT I WAS GOING PLACES.
I WANTED TO BE THE PROTAGONIST OF A TRIUMPHANT STORY.
NO.
THIS ISN'T IT.
DON'T STOP!
I...
I COULD...
HAVE DONE SO MUCH MORE ...!!

ABOUT THINGS I ASPIRED TO.
BUT...
REALITY IS HARSH.

THIS IS THE WORLD I DREAMED OF.
Next up...
giving a farewell performance on behalf of the modern music club...
AH!
Ashie Taiyou-kun!
MY DAY-DREAMS WERE ALL...

MY FINGERS...
ARE ELECTRIC!
THEY'RE DANCING!
THIS IS SO MUCH FUN!!
MY VOICE...
I HEAR IT.
EVERY-ONE'S...
CHEERING!

WHAT AN INCRED-IBLE...
VIEW.
IT'S FAN-TASTIC!

"It's a cheer-up charm.
"My mom showed me how to do it.
"Like this.
DON'T CRY!
"If you clench your fist...
CRY!
"then every-thing will be all right."
Next up...
giving a farewell performance on behalf of the modern music club...
Ashie Taiyou-kun!
HUH?
OH...

WOW!
AWE-SOME!
I WISH I HAD A BAND.
I WONDER IF I COULD EVER BE AS COOL AS HIM.
HIKARI COULD PROBABLY PULL IT OFF.
"This guitar can draw out your true talent."
IT'S NOT A MAGIC GUITAR.
BUT THAT'S OKAY.
Do your best!
"Have you heard of this?

Do your best!
Next up, we have a special guest!
A local college band that's making waves!!

AH! IT TICKLES.
ALMOST DONE.
CLASP
CLOSE IT TIGHT!
DON'T LOOK YET!
KEEP IT CLOSED!
OKAY!
GO FOR IT!

ARE YOU DOING A COMEDY ROUTINE NOW?
HUH?
TAKE IT OFF!
THE GUITAR?
NO! THE BOWTIE, IDIOT!
Huh?! It's so fashionable though!
WHAT'S YOUR SETLIST FOR THE PERFORMANCE?
I'LL SING A LITTLE, BUT THE GUITAR SOLO WILL BE THE MAIN ATTRACTION!
COME CHECK IT OUT!
WEAR A NORMAL TIE!
c'mon!
That's all you've got to say?!
TAIYOU, WAIT.
GIVE ME YOUR HAND.

I DON'T REMEMBER MUCH ABOUT THE DAYS LEADING UP TO THE CULTURAL FESTIVAL.
PROBABLY NOTHING SPECIAL.
IT WAS JUST HECTIC.
I WISH I HAD MADE MORE MEMORIES BACK THEN.
WITH HIKARI...
AND SAKURA.
SPECIAL LIVE MUSIC 9/8
COMPETITION
DANCE COMPETITION
HIGH CULTURAL FESTIVAL 56
WELCOME
GENERAL INFORMATION
Cultural Festival Hours
9/8 (Sat)
General Admission
9:30-4:00
9/9 (Sun)

NO WAY!
NOT A CHANCE!
I KNOW I WAS A PAIN IN THE ASS.
BUT I NEEDED YOU.
IF POSSIBLE...
I WANTED TO BE YOUR FRIEND FOREVER.

GOOD MORNING, HIKARI!
GUESS I CAN'T GIVE UP AFTER ALL!
I WANNA MAKE MUSIC WITH YOU, NO MATTER WHAT!!
WHAT IS YOUR PROB-LEM?!
CAN'T YOU TAKE A HINT?!
I'LL PERFORM AT THE CULTURAL FESTIVAL BY MYSELF.
SO...
WATCH ME!
ONCE YOU SEE WHAT I CAN DO...
I *KNOW* YOU'LL WANNA FORM A BAND WITH ME!

NOT FRIENDS. YOU'RE NOTHING TO ME.
I HAD NO IDEA ABOUT WHY YOUR FINGERS WOULDN'T MOVE...
OR WHY YOU HATED PEOPLE...
OR WHEN YOUR BIRTH-DAY WAS...
OR WHERE YOU LIVED.
YET I ALREADY THOUGHT OF YOU AS A FRIEND.
IT'S A BAD HABIT OF MINE.
I'LL NEVER FORGET YOUR FACE THAT DAY.

I DON'T KNOW WHAT TO SAY.
WOULD ...
WOULD IT BE OKAY TO ASK HIM WHY HIS FINGERS CAN'T MOVE?
DO YOU SEE NOW?
I CAN'T DO IT.
I CAN'T EVEN PLAY THE PIANO ANYMORE.
SO QUIT BOTHERING ME.
DON'T TALK TO ME EVER AGAIN.
WE'RE...

HIS FINGERS AREN'T MOVING ...?
THEY ARE, BUT THE RING FINGER AND PINKY ON HIS LEFT HAND DON'T MOVE VERY WELL.
SOME-TIMES THEY TREMBLE OR LOOK LIKE THEY'LL SLIDE.
I CAN SEE HOW THAT WOULD MAKE PERFORMING DIFFICULT.
SOME-TIMES HE PAUSES...
BUT IT'S STILL CLEAR HE'S BETTER THAN ME.

SO THIS IS YOUR GUITAR?
YEAH.
MY OLD MAN GAVE IT TO ME.
Cute, ain't it?!
I'VE BEEN USING IT FOR MUSIC CLUB.
GO AHEAD AND GIVE IT A STRUM!
IT MIGHT HURT YOUR EARS.
IT WON'T!
MY FINGERS ARE A BIT STIFF.

YESTERDAY, I SAID SOME MEAN STUFF SO YOU'D LEAVE ME ALONE...
You did?!
HOW CAN YOU ACT LIKE NOTHING HAPPENED?
YOU REALLY ARE AN IDIOT.
UM, WELL-- I WASN'T SURE ABOUT WHAT TO SAY TO YOU TODAY...
BUT...
I CAN'T GIVE UP ON YOU, HIKARI.
I'M THE TYPE THAT, IF CHANCES ARE HIGHER THAN ZERO, I CAN'T GIVE UP.
They are zero.
BECAUSE OF YOU, HIKARI, I COULDN'T SLEEP LAST NIGHT.
I EVEN DRANK COFFEE!
It was just the coffee.
WOULD YOU GIVE UP IF YOU HEARD ME PLAY GUITAR?
I WANNA HEAR YOU PLAY!!
BUT I STILL WON'T GIVE UP!

STRIDE
スタ
スタ
STRIDE
SAKURA, I'LL INTRODUCE YOU!
HE'S MY FRIEND!
Who?
HIKARI!
HOW ARE YA?!
I'm good, btw!!
THIS IS SAKURA! SHE LIVES NEAR ME!
WE'VE BEEN FRIENDS SINCE ELEMENTARY SCHOOL!
Now you two can be friends!
FWP
STRIDE
STRIDE
IS HE REALLY YOUR FRIEND?
He completely ignored you.
Yeah, he's my friend!
WELL, SORRY FOR BOTHERING YOU, SAKURA!
HAVE A GREAT DAY!
HIKARI, WAIT!
HIKARI, WHERE DO YOU LIVE?!
WE WERE IN THE SAME JUNIOR HIGH, SO YOU MUST LIVE IN THE SAME AREA, RIGHT?!
WHAT ABOUT ELEMENTARY--

MORNING!!
TAKING PHOTOS OF YOUR NAME-SAKE?
Ah ha ha!
I'M SO GLAD!
I WAS AFRAID YOU HAD QUIT PHOTO-GRAPHY COM-PLETELY!
That's great! I love seeing you taking photos more than any-thing!!
...
AH HA HA!
SAKURA'S SMILE IS ENOUGH TO MAKE ME HAPPY.
WHAT'S SO FUNNY?
I CAN'T BELIEVE HOW HYPER YOU ARE IN THE MORNINGS.
HUH?
AH!
HIKARI!

SECRETS...
WHAT KIND OF SECRETS COULD A GUY HAVE?
......
I FEEL LIKE CRAP.
WHAT SHOULD I SAY TO HIM TOMORROW?
Taiyou, knock it off with the guitar!
Shouldn't you be studying?!
SAKURA!

I ONLY EVER THOUGHT ABOUT MYSELF.
I NEVER EVEN CONSIDERED...
WHAT OTHERS WERE THINKING.
WHAT THEY WERE FEELING...
WHAT BURDENS THEY WERE CARRYING.
I DIDN'T WANT TO FEEL THE PAIN OTHERS WERE DEALING WITH.
If...
you were to learn my secret...
all of your talent would disappear.
All you have gained would be **lost.**
So don't stick your nose into my business.

SO THAT'S IT.
IS THIS UNDER-CLASSMAN A GUY?
YEAH.
AND DO YOU... LIKE HIM?
YEAH.
WELL, GOOD LUCK WITH ENTRANCE EXAMS.
MAKE SURE YOU ACTUALLY STUDY. DON'T JUST PLAY YOUR GUITAR THE WHOLE TIME!
I SHOULD HAVE TOLD HER.

COULD I REALLY TELL HER...
THAT I WANTED TO GO TO TOKYO TOGETH-ER?
SAKURA...
DID SOMETHING HAPPEN?
YEAH... I GUESS ...
AN...
AN UNDER-CLASSMAN IN THE PHOTO-GRAPHY CLUB...
SAID I SHOULDN'T GO TO TOKYO.
WHAT?

I'VE BEEN THINKING ABOUT NOT GOING TO COLLEGE.
HUH?
YOU'RE NOT... GOING TO TOKYO?
NOPE.
WHAT ABOUT YOU?
ARE YOU GOING TO SCHOOL IN TOKYO?
WELL... I'VE GOT AN IDEA OF WHERE I WANNA GO...
BUT ONLY BECAUSE ...
SAKURA SAID SHE WANTED TO GO TO TOKYO.
SO YOU'RE NOT GONNA STUDY PHOTO-GRAPHY?
NAH.
I'M OVER THAT.
WHY... DID IT CHANGE SO QUICKLY?
SAKURA'S ACTING STRANGE.
HEY.

SAKURA!
GONNA WALK HOME WITH YOUR BOY-FRIEND?
He's *not* my boy-friend!!
YOU PICK A COLLEGE YET?
NAH.
THERE ARE PLENTY OF PLACES YOU CAN STUDY PHOTOGRAPHY, RIGHT?
HAVE YOU LOOKED?
I DON'T KNOW A LOT ABOUT THESE THINGS, BUT I'M HERE IF YOU WANNA TALK.

JUST... GIVE IT UP ALREADY.
THINKING BACK, I SHOULDN'T HAVE HASSLED HIM SO MUCH.
HE STILL HAD...
SO MANY SECRETS.

QUIT BUGGING ME.
GIVE IT A TRY!
I WON'T !!
NOT EVER AGAIN!!
YOU...
HAVE NO TALENT.

YOU DID THE ACCOMPANI-MENT FOR THE SCHOOL CONCERT EVERY YEAR.
IT BLEW MY MIND HOW TALENTED YOU WERE!
THAT'S WHY I WANT YOU...
TO PLAY AT THE CULTURAL FESTIVAL WITH ME!
PIANO? GUITAR? IT DOESN'T MATTER!
I'LL HANDLE THE SINGING, SO WHATEVER YOU WANT--
I'M NOT DOING IT.
WHY NOT?
HOW LONG HAS IT BEEN SINCE YOU PLAYED GUITAR?
I WANNA HEAR YOU PLAY AGAIN, HIKARI!
JUST STOP!

HMM.
YOUR RHYTHM'S UNEVEN.
YOUR CHORD PROGRES-SION IS SLOW.
I DON'T KNOW IF YOU'RE A BEGINNER OR WHAT, BUT YOU NEED MORE PRACTICE.
HIKARI?
DO YOU PLAY GUITAR?
NO.
BUT I'VE TRIED IT.
WHAT ABOUT PIANO?
YOU PLAYED IN JUNIOR HIGH, RIGHT?

HOW DID YOU FIND ME?
IT TOOK ME TWO YEARS TO FIND THIS HIDING SPOT.
WELL, I JUST SEARCHED THE ENTIRE SCHOOL!
What is this place? A supply closet?
WILL YOU LISTEN TO ME PLAY?
WHY ME...?
WHO SAID YOU COULD SIT THERE?
SERI-OUSLY?
THIS SUCKS. NOW I GOTTA FIND A NEW SPOT.
I'LL NEVER FIND ANYWHERE THIS GOOD--
TWANG
IF YOU HAVE NO PLACE TO GO...
COME WITH ME, MY BRO.
DON'T SING IT.
HANG OUT IN THE MODERN MUSIC CLUB-ROOM.
I TOLD YOU, I'M NOT JOINING.

Who...
are you?
That I can't tell you.
It's a secret.
If I told you...
If you told me...?
THERE YOU ARE, HIKARI!!
FLINCH
Listen to *this*!

No.
You have talent.
It's just hidden away.
This guitar can draw out your true skill.
This guitar can do *that?*
Wow...
It must be a magic guitar!
Yup.
As long as you use it correctly...
it can make your dreams come true.

JOIN THE MODERN MUSIC CLUB!
Hell no.
ISN'T THAT HIKARI-KUN?
WHO'S HE TALKING TO?
HE AND I ENDED UP IN THE SAME CLASS WHEN WE BECAME THIRD YEARS.
HE SAT IN THE BACK BY THE WINDOW. HE HARDLY TALKED TO ANYONE.
HE WAS PRETTY MYSTERI-OUS.
But...
I'm not very good at playing guitar...
I'm in the modern music club, but everyone just laughs at me.

IT'S HIKARI!
HIKARI?
BUT DON'T USE MY GIVEN NAME.
IT'S SO GIRLY.
CAN I CALL YOU HIKARI THEN?
I just told you *not* to!
HIKARI!
LET'S START A BAND TOGETHER!

GRAB
HIKARU-KUN!
WRONG.
HUH?!
AREN'T YOU TSUKIMOTO HIKARU-KU--
NO.

ダ DASH
?!
ダ DASH
?!
ビュ～ン ZWOOM
OH!
WAS THAT TSUKI-MOTO?
WHY'S HE RUNNING?
TSUKI-MOTO!

SHFF
SHFF
?
SHWAP
SHWAP
SHWF
BANDMATES WANTED!!
GRAB
GRIN

HE'S IN MY CLASS!
UH, HIS NAME IS...
OH, THANKS.
HEY, UM...
HERE, TAKE ONE!
SHWP

SOUNDS FUN, BUT...
I CAN'T PLAY ANY INSTRU-MENTS. SORRY!
SORRY, MY MAN!
I'VE GOT A GIRL-FRIEND NOW--
So what?!
Go brag some-where else!!
CRAP, NO ONE'S INTERESTED.
THEY WON'T EVEN LOOK AT MY FLYERS...
ビュウ
WHOOO
AH!
FLAP
ぱしっ
BANDMATES WANTED!!!
People Who Can Play Instruments
Anything's fine
CONTACT

TWAAANG
THAT'S RIGHT!
IT'S NOT OVER YET!
ALL I'VE GOTTA DO IS RECRUIT NEW MEMBERS.
THEN WE'LL **DEFINITELY** PLAY AT THE CULTURAL FESTIVAL!!
I'M NOT GIVING UP!!
PLEASE TAKE ONE!
BANDMATES WANTED!!
I BET YOU'D BE A GREAT BASSIST!
WANNA BE IN A BAND?
WHAT ARE YOU DOING, TAIYOU?
WANNA JOIN THE MODERN MUSIC CLUB?!
Nah, I'm on the baseball team.

DREAMS ARE JUST FANTASIES.
REALITY HAS ALWAYS LET ME DOWN.
IN MY THIRD YEAR OF HIGH SCHOOL...
I RAN INTO THIS MYSTERIOUS DUDE.
HE JUST SUDDENLY APPEARED BEFORE ME OUT OF THIN AIR.
HE SHOWED UP DURING MY DARKEST HOUR.
WAS HE AN ANGEL OR...A DEVIL?
C'MON, HE TOTALLY LOOKS LIKE A DEVIL.
THE STRANGER GAVE ME A GUITAR.
"USE THIS GUITAR...
"AND YOU'LL ENSNARE THE HEARTS OF ALL WHO HEAR IT."

WE ONLY JUST STARTED OUR THIRD YEAR!
AT LEAST STICK AROUND UNTIL SUMMER.
WE'LL DO A FAREWELL SHOW AT THE CULTURAL FEST.
BUT WE'VE GOT ENTRANCE EXAMS.
AND BEING IN THE SCHOOL'S MUSIC CLUB EATS UP SO MUCH TIME.
RIGHT. TAIYOU, AREN'T YOU GOING TO COLLEGE?
IT'S NOT THAT WE *WANT* TO BREAK UP THE BAND...
BUT WE NEED TO FOCUS ON OUR STUDIES NOW.
THERE ARE NO OTHER CLUB MEMBERS AND OUR SCHOOL ADVISOR IS M.I.A.!
GUESS THE MUSIC CLUB IS KINDA DEAD NOW.
SORRY, BUT WE CAN'T HELP YOU WITH YOUR DREAMS, MAN.
I mean, it's not like any of us have talent anyway.
AH HA HA HA!
B-BUT...

IN MY DAY-DREAMS...
I'M ALWAYS THE STAR.
SO, TODAY...
IS OUR LAST PRACTICE.
WELL, WE NEVER GOT TO PERFORM LIVE...
BUT IT WAS FUN!
AT LEAST WE GAVE IT OUR ALL!
ALL RIGHT, DISMISSED!
W-WAIT!!

MY SPECIAL TALENT IS DAY-DREAMING.
I OFTEN CREATE STORIES IN MY MIND.
I'M DEFINITELY BETTER AT THAT THAN I AM PLAYING THE GUITAR.
MY NAME IS ASHIE TAIYOU.
I'M A SENIOR IN HIGH SCHOOL.
ACTU-ALLY...
I HAVE A CONFES-SION.

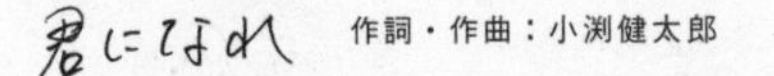

はやく大人になりたいのに 背を丸めていた頃がある
早送りも 巻き戻しも 出来ない時を 描きながら 生きてる
ヘタクソな今日の自分も 消さずに 上から あるがままを 描き足すだけ
大人になれば なるほど 空が 高く 高く 感じる

今はまだ 勝てなくて良い 負ける意味を 知る時だ
今はまだ 分からなくて良い 無理に飲み込んで 吐きだした 苦い想い
今はまだ 出来なくて良い 出来ない時にだけ 出来る事がある
今はまだ 迷えば良い どれを選んでも 君の答えなんだと 胸を張って言えるなら

今はまだ 会えなくて良い 会えない分だけ 強く想えれば良い
今はまだ 言えなくて良い 言えない程 大切な気持ちなんだろう
今はまだ 孤独で良い 未だ見ぬ仲間達も みんな 今 孤独だから
今はまだ そこにいれば良い 次の場所は 自分で 決めるんだ
今はまだ 何も無くて良い 空っぽなら 素直になれ
今はまだ そのままで良い 変わらないもの 守り続けながら 変われるなら

そんな君が 素敵かどうか？を 決めるのは 君じゃない
君を愛する人が 見てるのは 今よりもずっと遠くの君

駄目な時も 輝く時も 同じ様に 君を信じてる
その愛は 本物だから いつの日か 本物の君になれ

今はまだ 勝てなくて良い 分からなくて良い 出来なくて良い
迷えば良い 会えなくて良い 言えなくて良い 孤独で良い
今はまだ そこにいれば良い 何も無くて良い そのままで良い
いつの日か 本物の 君になれ
君になれ 君になれ

Note: See page 190 for transliteration and English lyrics.

TRACK1
Ashie
Taiyou

ASHIE TAIYOU, SEVEN-TEEN YEARS OLD.
STRENGTHS: ENERGETIC, POSITIVE, NEVER GIVES UP.
WEAK-NESSES: OBNOXIOUS, STUPID, DOESN'T KNOW WHEN TO GIVE UP.
BIGGEST DREAM: TO BE A MUSICIAN.
TRACK1